KU-719-694

What About Health?

Hygiene

by Cath Senker

HODDER
Wayland

an imprint of Hodder Children's Books

Titles in the WHAT ABOUT HEALTH? series

Drugs

Exercise

Food

Hygiene

Hygiene is a simplified version of the title
Hygiene and Your Health in Wayland's 'Health Matters' series.

Language level consultant: Norah Granger
Editor: Belinda Hollyer
Designer: Jane Hawkins

Text copyright 2001 Hodder Wayland
Volume copyright 2001 Hodder Wayland

First published in 2001 by Hodder Wayland,
an imprint of Hodder Children's Books.

British Library Cataloguing in Publication Data
Senker, Cath
Hygiene. - (What about health?)
1.Hygiene - Juvenile literature
I.Title
613.4
ISBN 0 7502 3609 4

Printed in Hong Kong

Hodder Children's Books
A division of Hodder Headline Ltd
338 Euston Road, London NW1 3BH

Picture acknowledgements
Illustrations: Jan Sterling
Cover: Hodder Wayland Picture Library (except bacteria, Stockmarket Photo Agency); Chris Fairclough
Colour Library 7, 25 top; Northern Picture Library 13; Reflections 15 top; Science Photo Library 5, 15
bottom, 23 bottom, 27, 28 (S. Nagendra); Tony Stone Worldwide 17 bottom (Lori Adamski Peek), 19
(Andrew Syned), 23 top (David Oliver), 25 (MacNeal Hospital), 26 (John Fortunato), 29 bottom (David
Austen); Hodder Wayland Picture Library 4, 6 (both), 8, 10, 11, 12, 14, 16, 17 top, 18, 19 bottom, 20, 22
middle; Zefa 9, 21 both, 24, 29 top (H. Sochurek).

Contents

What is hygiene?   4

Now wash your hands!   6

Clean skin   8

Smelling fresh   10

Strong white teeth   12

Shiny clean hair   14

Changing your clothes   16

Hygiene at home   18

Safe, fresh food   20

Clean, healthy pets   22

Accidents and hygiene   24

Germs and illness   26

Fighting disease   28

Glossary   30

Finding out more   31

Index   32

What is hygiene?

Hygiene is about keeping our bodies and our homes clean. If you keep your body clean, you can help to fight off germs.

There are different kinds of germs. Bacteria are tiny living things that live all around us. Some bacteria can make you ill. Viruses are the tiniest germs. They can infect the cells in the body and cause disease.

Wash your face and brush your teeth to keep them clean. ▶

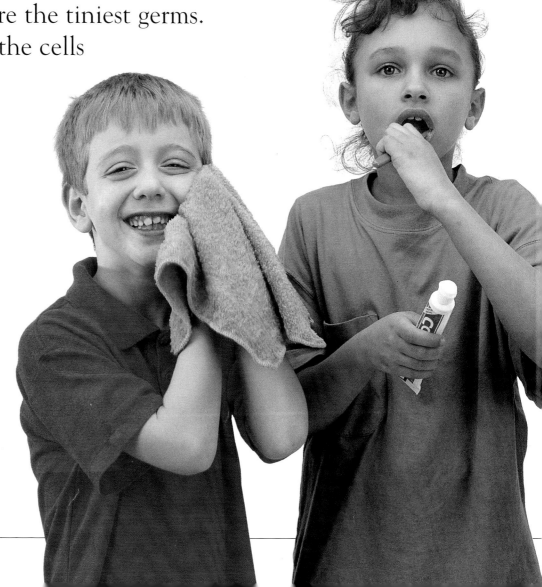

HOW YOUR BODY FIGHTS OFF GERMS

BREATHING SYSTEM
The lining of your nose and windpipe traps germs.

SKIN
Your skin keeps out germs. It repairs itself when you are cut.

STOMACH
Chemicals here can kill bacteria.

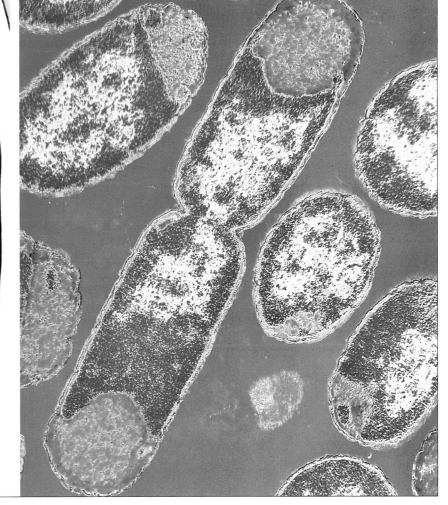

This picture of bacteria was taken through a microscope. Bacteria grow quickly in warm and wet places. ▶

Now wash your hands!

You should wash your hands often so that you don't spread germs.

Always wash your hands before you eat. If you have dirty hands, harmful bacteria might get on to your food and make you ill.

▲ Use a nailbrush to clean under your nails.

Remember to wash your hands after going to the toilet or touching a pet.

Keep your fingernails short so that no dirt can get stuck underneath them.

Wash your hands with soap and warm water. ▶

HANDY RULES

Wash your hands –

● Before touching food
● After going to the toilet
● After touching pets

These children will wash their hands after planting seeds. ▶

People who work with food have to keep their hands clean all the time. You could make a poster to remind them to wash their hands.

Clean skin

Your skin helps to stop germs from getting inside your body.

Your skin is always growing. Your body makes new skin cells, and the dead skin cells come off. When you have a bath or shower, you wash away dead skin cells, dirt and bacteria.

▲ A sponge helps to scrub away dead skin.

It helps to have a bath or shower every day.▼

◀ Muslims washing before they pray. Washing is important in many religions. Hindus also wash as part of their worship, and Christians are baptised with water.

KEEP CLEAN

- Try to wash all over every day
- Try to have a bath or shower after doing sports

Smelling fresh

As you get older, you sweat more. If you don't wash away the sweat, your skin can start to smell.

You sweat most on your hands and feet, under your arms and between your legs. Try to wash these parts of your body twice a day, and always after doing sports.

Athlete's foot and verrucas are skin infections. You can catch them in damp places like swimming pools. Look after your feet by washing and drying them carefully.▼

CLOSE-UP OF A SWEAT GLAND

Sweating cools you down. The sweat goes into the air, carrying away body heat.

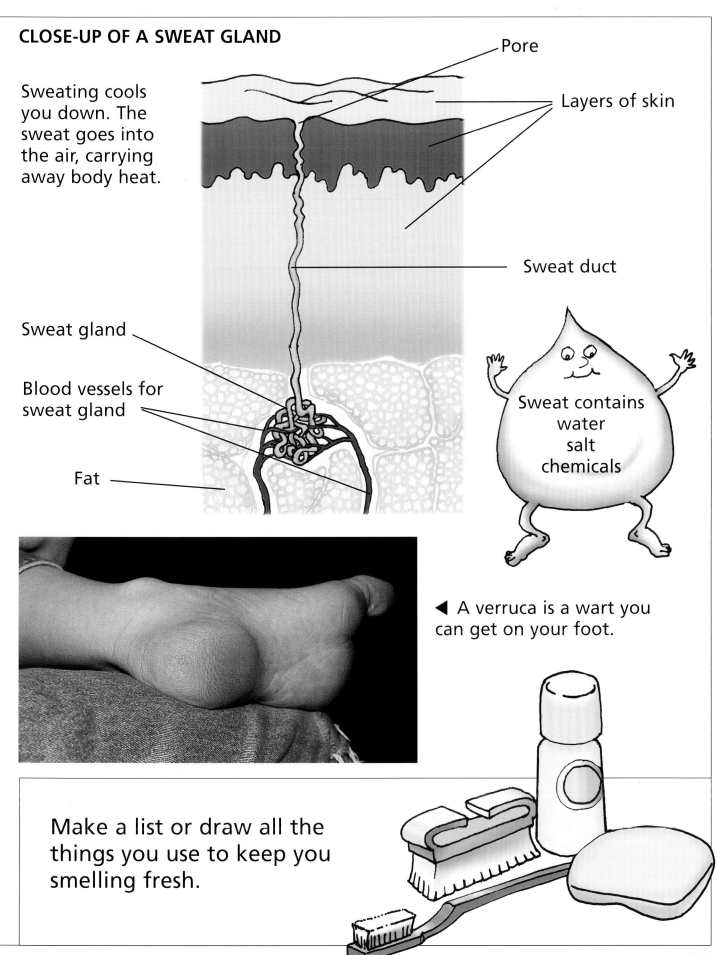

Pore

Layers of skin

Sweat duct

Sweat gland

Blood vessels for sweat gland

Fat

Sweat contains
water
salt
chemicals

◀ A verruca is a wart you can get on your foot.

Make a list or draw all the things you use to keep you smelling fresh.

Strong white teeth

At about six years old, you grow new teeth. Look after them – they have to last you all your life.

When you eat something sweet, bacteria in your mouth eat up the sugar and make acid. If you eat lots of sweet things, the acid can damage the hard coating on your teeth and make a hole in it. Then you will need to have a filling.

Crunchy foods like apples and carrots are good for your teeth.

◀ Try to brush your teeth twice a day. If you can't brush, rinse your mouth with water instead.

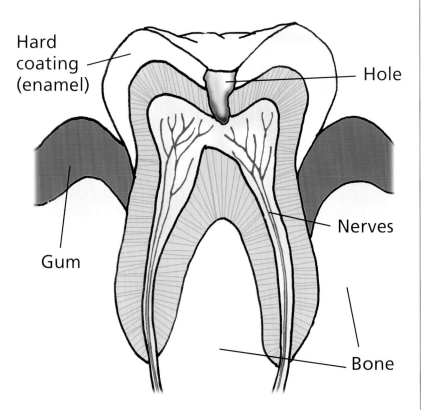

Hard coating (enamel)

Hole

Nerves

Gum

Bone

CLOSE-UP OF A TOOTH WITH A HOLE

▲ Try not to eat too many sugary foods, or you might get holes in your teeth.

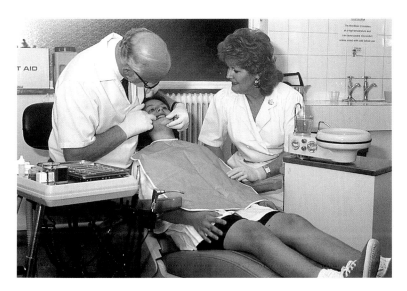

▲ Visit your dentist for a check-up every six months.

BRUSHING TEETH

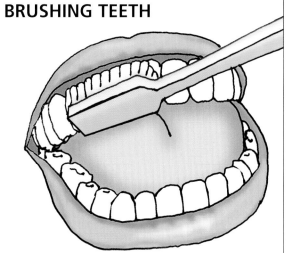

1. Clean the outside and inside of your top teeth.

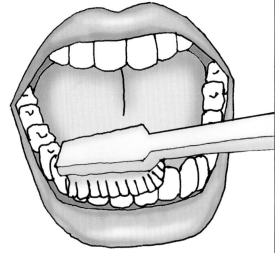

2. Clean the outside and inside of your bottom teeth.

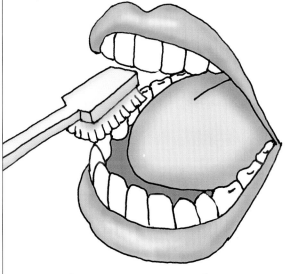

3. Brush the biting surfaces.

Shiny clean hair

Try to wash your hair every few days. Make sure you rinse it well after you shampoo.

The skin on your head makes oil, which helps your hair to look shiny. As you grow up, your skin may make more oil. The oil can make your hair greasy, and you may have to wash it more often.

◀ Use a gentle shampoo on your hair.

▲ Wash your brush and comb every week.

CLOSE-UP OF A HAIR

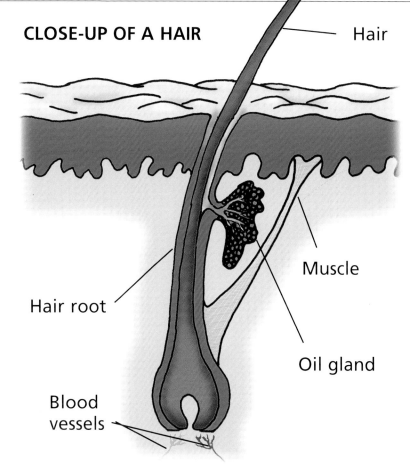

Hair

Muscle

Hair root

Oil gland

Blood vessels

Head lice are tiny insects that can live in your hair and make your head itchy. If people catch head lice, they can use a nit comb or special shampoo to get rid of them.

Close-up of a louse around a hair. ▶

▲ Comb away lice and their eggs (called nits) with a nit comb.

15

Changing your clothes

Hygiene means changing your clothes regularly as well as washing your body.

Sweat and bacteria build up in your clothes as the day goes on. Your clothes can start to smell, especially in hot weather. It's best to wear cotton underwear to keep you feeling fresh. Remember to change your underwear every day.

Clothes need washing regularly. ▶

◀Cotton material has tiny holes that let the air reach your body. The air helps your body to get rid of sweat.

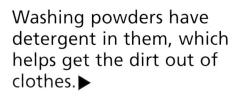

Washing powders have detergent in them, which helps get the dirt out of clothes.▶

◀ You sweat when you do sport, so wash your kit after each game.

Hygiene at home

In a dirty home, bacteria and tiny insects called dust mites can make people ill.

Bacteria grow quickly in warm, damp places, so kitchens and bathrooms need to be clean. Dust mites live in carpets and bedclothes. Dusting and vacuuming regularly gets rid of them. It helps to change your bedclothes every week, too.

Detergent loosens bits of food from dishes.▼

If you have an allergy to dust mites, you may itch or sneeze a lot. ▶

◄ Close-up of a dust mite. Dust mites feed on people's dead skin.

Vacuum up dust with a vacuum cleaner. ►

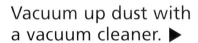

Make a collage with pictures of things that are used to keep homes clean.

Safe, fresh food

If you touch food with dirty hands, you will put germs on it. The germs could make you ill. Raw foods like fruit may have dirt and poisonous chemicals on them. They should be washed before you eat them.

Bacteria grow where it is warm and damp. If you keep fresh foods in the fridge, it is harder for bacteria to grow.

Some foods, such as meat and eggs, need to be cooked right through to kill harmful bacteria.

▲ Some foods are canned, frozen or dried to stop bacteria from growing on them.

Food will stay fresh for longer in the fridge. ▶

FOODS THAT CAN HAVE HARMFUL BACTERIA

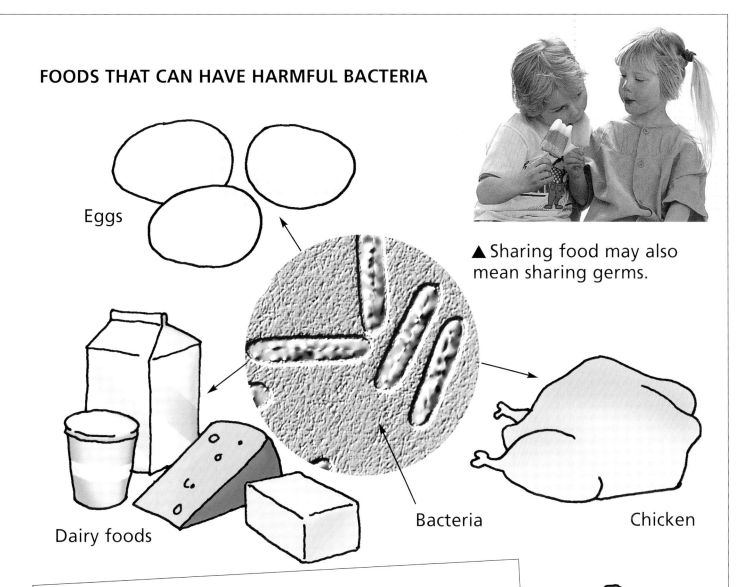

Eggs

Dairy foods

Bacteria

Chicken

▲ Sharing food may also mean sharing germs.

FOOD HYGIENE
- Wash your hands before touching food
- Keep flies and pets away from food
- Eat food before the 'use by' date

Cover a slice of bread and a cup of milk and leave them in a warm place for a few days. Check them each day. What happens? Can you find out why?

Clean, healthy pets

Pets need to be clean, too. Cats wash themselves, but dogs should be bathed. Comb your cat's or dog's coat to get rid of old fur, and check for fleas.

Use flea powder to kill the fleas. ▼

Give your pet fresh food and water every day. Your pet should have a clean place to sleep, too. Cage animals need fresh straw or paper, so change it regularly.

▲ These children will wash their hands after playing with the rabbit.

◀ Pets should be cleaned out regularly.

You can sometimes catch a skin infection called ringworm from animals. A special cream will get rid of it. ▶

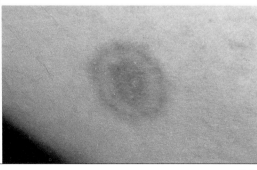

Accidents and hygiene

If you cut yourself, keep the broken skin really clean to stop germs from getting into your body.

Wash the cut under running water, then put on antiseptic cream. You may need a plaster or bandage. If you have a deep cut, you might need stitches.

Put a plaster on a cut to keep it clean.▼

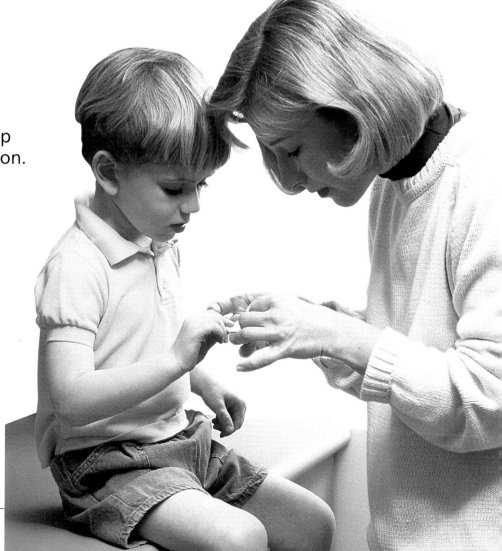

Tiny white blood cells help your body to fight infection.
▼

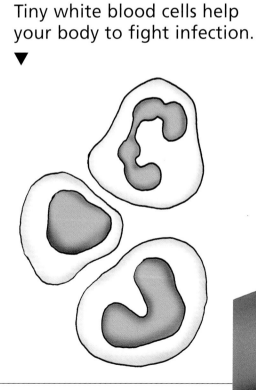

If you burn yourself, hold the skin under cold running water for ten minutes. Then cover it.

▲ A bandage keeps out germs.

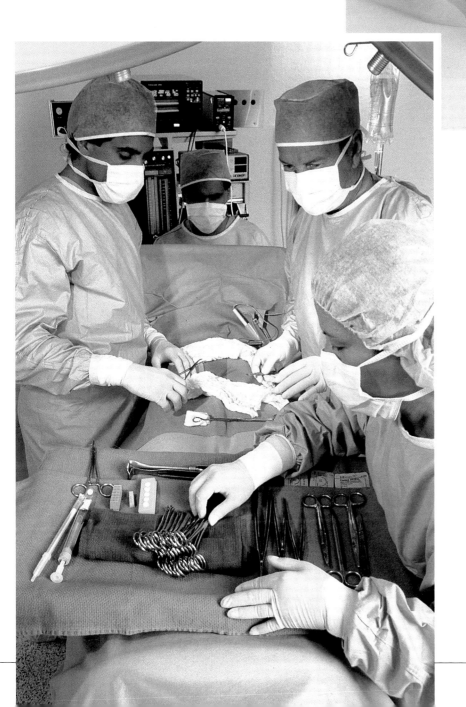

◄ During an operation in hospital, everything is kept clean and free of germs.

Germs and illness

If germs get into your body, they can make you ill.

A cold is a virus. When you catch a cold, your nose is runny with mucus. Your body is trying to wash out the virus with the mucus. You cough and sneeze so that you can breathe more easily.

You spread germs when you sneeze. It's better to use a tissue!
▼

◀ With a bad cold, you might have a temperature.

When you are ill, your body needs energy to fight the germs. Try to rest, keep warm and drink lots of water.

HOW INFECTIONS CAN SPREAD

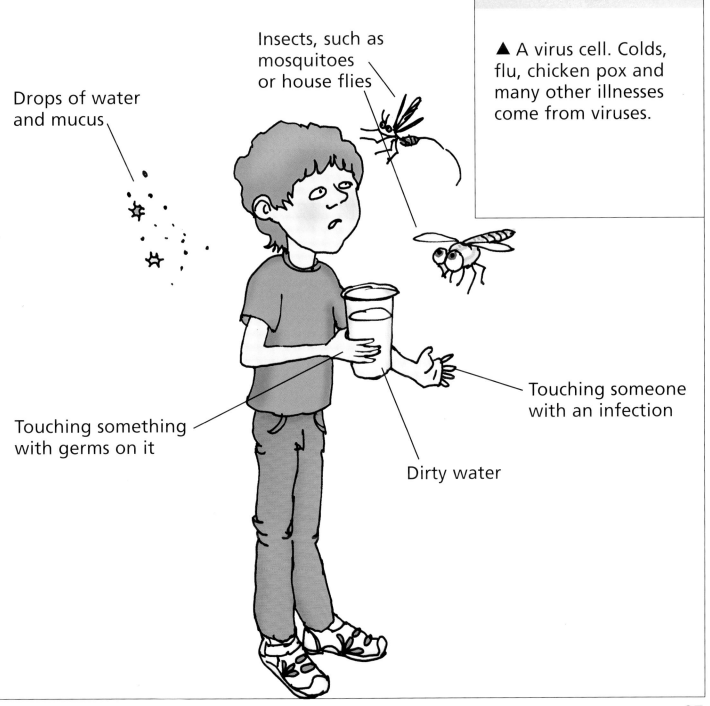

▲ A virus cell. Colds, flu, chicken pox and many other illnesses come from viruses.

Drops of water and mucus

Insects, such as mosquitoes or house flies

Touching something with germs on it

Dirty water

Touching someone with an infection

Fighting disease

Hygiene is important to stop diseases from spreading.

You can also be immunized to stop you from getting some diseases. A weak form of the disease is injected into you, or given to you in a drink. Your body makes antibodies to kill it. If you come into contact with the disease again, you won't catch it.

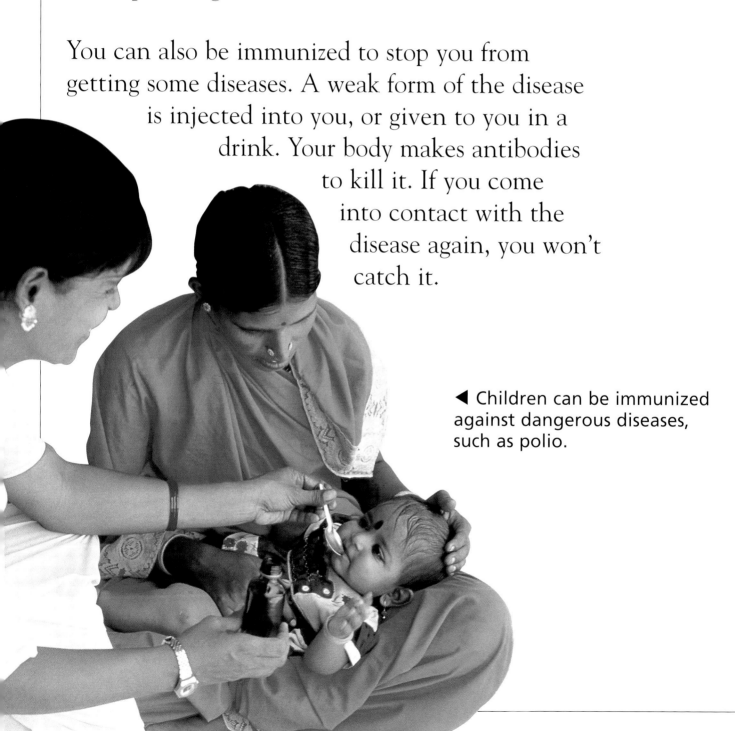

◄ Children can be immunized against dangerous diseases, such as polio.

This is the HIV virus seen through a microscope. HIV can cause the disease called AIDS. This stops people's bodies from fighting infections.▶

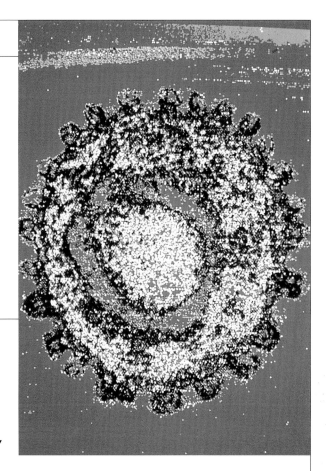

Children in Thailand collecting clean water. Using clean water helps to prevent disease.▼

Glossary

Allergy If you become ill when you come into contact with certain foods, dust, or pollen from flowers, you have an allergy.

Antibodies Germ-killers in your body.

Antiseptic A medicine that kills germs.

Bacteria Tiny living things. Some are useful but others can cause illnesses.

Blood vessels Tubes that carry blood all around your body.

Germs Bacteria or viruses that can cause disease.

Gland A cell in your body that makes oil, sweat or other substances.

Immunized Given an injection or a drink to prevent disease.

Infections Illnesses caused by germs getting into your body.

Temperature You have a temperature when your body is hotter than normal.

Verruca A wart that grows underneath your foot. A wart is a small, hard growth caused by a virus.

Virus A tiny germ that can infect the cells in your body and make it ill.

Windpipe The tube that carries air from your throat to your lungs.

Finding out more

BOOKS TO READ

Diet and Health by Alison Dalgleish and Rachel Fuller
(Hodder Wayland, 1997)

Head Lice by Allison Lassieur (Watts, 2000)

Professor Protein's Fitness, Health, Hygiene and Relaxation Tonic
by Steve Parker and Rob Shone (Aladdin, 1996)

Tooth Decay and Cavities by Alvin Silverstein (Watts, 1999)

VIDEOS

Crunch Time: Dental Health (Channel Four Schools, 1999)
How diet, personal hygiene and visiting the dentist help keep teeth healthy

Look Who's Growing Up! (Rainbow Educational Video, USA, 1997)
About puberty, including healthy living and hygiene

ORGANIZATIONS

Health Development Agency
(this used to be called the Health Education Authority)
Trevelyan House, 30 Great Peter Street,
London SW1P 2HW.
Telephone 020 7222 5300
Website www.hea.org.uk

Index

AIDS 29
allergy 18
antiseptic 24

bacteria 4, 5, 6, 8, 12, 16, 18, 20, 21
bathrooms 18
blood 24
burns 25

cotton 16, 17
cuts 24

detergent 17, 18
dirt 6, 8, 17, 18, 20
disease 4, 28, 29
disinfectants 18
dust 18, 19

fleas 22
food 6, 7, 12, 18, 20, 21, 22

germs 4, 5, 6, 8, 20, 21, 24,
  25, 26, 27
glands   11

hair 14, 15
head lice 15

infection 10, 23, 26, 27
insects 15, 18, 19, 21, 22, 27

kitchens 18, 21

oil 14

pets 6, 7, 21, 22, 23
pores 11

religion 9

skin 14
skin cells 8, 10
smell 10, 16
sports 10, 17
sweat 10, 11, 16, 17

teeth 12, 13
toilet 6, 7

vacuuming 18, 19
virus 4, 26, 27, 29

washing 6, 7, 8, 9, 10, 14, 15, 16, 17, 18,
  20, 21, 23, 24
water for drinking 23, 27, 29
white blood cells 24